D0107755

BECAUSE I SAID SO....LESSONS FROM AN ITALIAN MOM
A COLLECTION OF LESSONS, ADVICE AND JUST
BECAUSES

by

Pamela A. Costa

Dedication

This book is dedicated to all the amazing Italian mothers who came before me. The Italian women who love and live passionately and teach us everyday to do the same. To my own Italian Mother who has taught me so many life lessons and encourages me everyday to do and be everything I can. To my children who are beautiful inside and out. I love you past heaven. My amazing husband who supports every wild and crazy idea I have. I love you completely.

I very special thank you to Letizia Bologna who I admire all the time. Love you sister.

BECAUSE I SAID SO....LESSONS FROM AN ITALIAN MOM
A COLLECTION OF LESSONS, ADVICE AND JUST
BECAUSES

I have so much to say, I don't know where to begin. Of course
I have a lot to say, I am Italian. Now, I am not 100% Italian,
but you would never know that. I am 50% Italian and the rest
is Irish, Scottish, German, yada, yada, yada...but trust me, I
am Italian. My mother is 100% Italian and taught me
everything I needed to know. I am going to give you advice,
teach you lessons and guide you through life. The Italian way.

I knew I could not write this book until I had visited the Motherland ---- Italy, with all it's glory, romance, art, religion, food and love. It consumes you and makes you want to be more Italian than you already are if that can be understood. Your senses are heightened and you become aware of the simple things. The things we take for granted in the United States are so meaningless. A simple meal with family is an art form. A walk to the square at midnight is more fulfilling than a trip to Disneyland. My husband and I danced in the middle of the square at midnight and we felt like teenagers in love again. This magical place is now my second home and it has made me understand my heritage and my passion for life more than any book or video or movie could have ever done. I walk down the middle of the streets and listen to the men and women talking with such passion, I now understand why I am so loud and opinionated. It is not because I feel I am right, it is because I am so passionate about what I believe.

The one thing I always look back on is how the Italians show love. It is as simple as passing around five small cups and sharing a drink. They do not have the "it's all mine" mentality. They share everything. They have family discussions and that is their form of entertainment. Material things are not what is important. They raise their children to be strong willed and hard workers. They teach love as an emotion not a physical act. Everything they do for one another is done with love with no expectations of getting anything in return.

This may be taken wrong, but I have to say it. On my first trip to Italy, I was very saddened over the treatment of women. It is very hard for them to find paying jobs. The man is dominant and the wage earner. Girls get married and are taken care of. Here in the United States, everyone one wants to be equal. I had opportunities that my Italian sisterhood does not have. I have a bachelors degree, a masters degree, a teaching credential and a career. But, I am proud that I take care of my family. I take care of the home. I take care of my husband. That is how they do it in Italy and I am perfectly fine doing that here. It's OK. Because I said so!

BOOK ONE, LESSON ONE, CHAPTER ONE (CALL IT WHATEVER YOU WANT)

......DATING, SHUT UP, YOU'RE NOT GONNA MARRY HIM!

Now let's set the record straight. I am not a doctor, a psychiatrist, a nurse, or any certified therapist. I am, however, a credentialed teacher, a successful event planner, a travel agent, and a wife married 25 years to an amazing man. But the one thing I am the most proud of is that I am a mother of two of the most incredible, kind-hearted, open-minded, amazing, loving, phenomenal kids to ever walk the face of the earth. Did I mention they are gorgeous? As an Italian mother, I am entitled to brag relentlessly about my children. That's what we do. Everyone asks me how did you raise two great kids? I am going to tell you, but it is going to take a while. So grab some vino and keep reading.

With the credentials I have, I feel I am entitled to share with you the things I know. I am an expert in my own universe. Hey, you bought this book, so you at least are curious about what I have to say. You may not agree with it, but too bad. The first topic I would like to cover is dating. Way back, long ago, when the dinosaurs roamed the earth, I dated. According to my husband, I dated 365 guys, which, is so far beyond the truth, it is hysterical. Now, remember my heritage. With that being said, puberty was so unkind to me, it hurt. First came the period. I remember the date and time like it was yesterday. I told my mother and the first thing out of her mouth was, "Where's the belt?" I started crying. "What belt?" In her day, they had pads and a belt. For God's sake mom, we have a new thing called adhesive, we don't need belts. My life was over.

The second my period started, the frizzy hair sprouted. The most uncontrollable, frizzy hair anyone has ever seen. My head looked like a Brillo Pad. I was then blessed with braces. Not the little, clear, square braces the kids have now. The shiny, metal wrap around braces of the 80's. They were connected with a wire that could tow a car. The icing on the cake was the headgear that had to be worn everyday. I was quite the looker. So, I did not date until my junior year. Of, course, I was the good Catholic girl, with LOADS of Catholic guilt. If i sinned in any way, shape or form, I was going to hell. Good Catholic girls - that is a whole other book.

My junior year was a learning year. I had an amazing friend, Leticia. She lived here, but her family was in Sicily. She is my sister. I have never thought of her as anything less. Talk about a cook, she is amazing. My heart was torn into a million pieces when she had to move back to Sicily. I threw her a going away party and cried through the whole thing. The one positive that came out of that party was my first love. He was a football player with a large family and through the years of on and off dating (there were 5), I came to find out that he had a huge drug problem. I was the good girl he took to all the family gatherings and holidays. His family loved me. Unfortunately, he was sleeping with all the bad girls. I found out about a few, but you know how first love goes, I forgave and forgave and then could not take it anymore. His drug problem was out of control by the 5th year. My parents found out and made me end it. I thought I could change him and I gave him the choice, me or the drugs…. I think you all know what he chose!! But I am so happy to say that he got help very soon after we broke up and he has a beautiful family today and I am very happy for him. He opened a very successful tile and granite company and I felt that he owed me big time. Needless to say, after my husband and I bought our first home, my kitchens and bathrooms were remodeled to the nines! At a very low cost!

My Senior year brought a wonderful baseball player that upped my popularity. This was an off year from the first love. I now had friends that never knew I existed until I dated the popular, baseball player. This wonderful popularity lasted my entire Senior year. Then poof, done. He was a cheater, too. After high school, I dated here and there. Went back to cheater number one quite a few times until I gave him "the choice". Here is where the lesson comes in.
ALWAYS LISTEN TO YOUR MOTHER, SHE IS ALWAYS RIGHT.

My Italian mother is 76 and I am 48 and I still listen to her. I still desperately want her approval. Had I listened to her, a whole lot of heartache would have been avoided. When I dated these boys, she preached to me that I did not know what love was, because I was going to marry everyone of them. She told me I wasn't going to marry them. If my mother had a dollar for everytime I told her she just did not understand, she could pay off the national debt. Really she could! My mother can see through bull shit like no other. I hate when she is right, which is 90% of the time. The other 10% when she is wrong, she is right in her head, so that makes her right all the time. It's crazy how she does it!

Here is an example of mother is always right. I met a guy who was slightly older and VERY charming. My mom did not like him at first sight. I was rebellious and determined to prove her wrong. We continued to date. He told me he was trying out for the Los Angeles Dodgers. I fell hook, line and sinker. I shared this with my friend who was a full blown Dodger fan. She informed me that he was full of it because the Dodgers were in Florida at spring training, Hmmmm. I later invited him to dinner for mom's homemade pizza. During dinner, the dumb ass asks my mother if she liked him. Without skipping a beat, she says no but that he could stay for dinner. I slithered under the table. Broke up with him later that night.

I learned through these dating adventures to always be who I was. I did not have to pretend to be someone that they wanted. I needed to be me. In Italy, if you are not married by the time you are in your early 20's, you are an old maid and no one will ever want you. Believe it or not, I believed that. Thank God I knew what I wanted early on. My mother taught me to not give a shit what other people thought. I applied that to my dating life and now my personal life and I was and am so much happier.

I look at the young girls today and just shake my head. They change who they are for the BOY they are dating. Daughters, listen to me: If they are the one, they are going to love you for who you are, not how high you can push up those boobies with that $75.00 bra from Victoria Secret. (I will cover shopping a few chapters ahead.) They are not not going to cheat on you because you tell them you love football and you ask them if the quarterback made a homerun. OK, maybe I did that, but just once.

When I met my husband, we had both come out of horrible relationships and I was not going to waste my time with someone who was not what I wanted. I had a list of questions that I asked him and he answered them all right. Piece of cake, he was the one. We dated three months, got engaged, married in a year and 25 years later, here we are. He is married to the Italian expert! Me!

On our first date, he took me to see Moonstruck, my ultimate favorite movie. When it gets to the part when Cher's boyfriend gets on one knee and proposes, I turned to him in the theater and said, that is how you are going to do it. And he did! You just know. Those of you with Italian mothers and grandmothers, you know they say that all the time. "You just know!"

Here is my list of extremely important questions to ask when you think you have met the one. I suggest you ask these within the first two weeks of dating so you don't waste your time.

1. Are you married?
2. Do you have children?
3. Do you practice a certain faith?
4. Do you believe in a 50/50 relationship?
5. Will I be able to stay home with our children?
6. Are you married? Really??
7. Are your parents still alive?
8. How far away does your psycho ex-girlfriend live?
9. Can you cook?
10. Are you married? Just tell me, you know I'll find out!

So, why do I harp on the married question? I have seen it too many times. Men love the chase. Single or married, it does not matter. I listen to these young girls, who fall in love with THE ONE only to find out he is married with three kids. The poor girl thinks and truly believes that the man is going to leave his wife for her. In the words of the wise CHER, "Snap out of it!" Ladies, you can't get a man to leave his wife. Stop trying to change him!

My Italian grandmother knew. She just knew. My mother was dating a guy. He was too good to be true. My grandmother could sniff out the crap in a heartbeat. So, one night, my grandmother wrote down the license plate of the jerk that was dating my mother. A simple call to her police officer and a promise of an Italian meal, and there you have it. He was married. She just knew. I think that is where I get my instincts. We have always said my mother is a witch because she just knows. Well, I guess I am a witch, too.

CHAPTER TWO - I MARRIED SANFORD

As an Italian wife, I enjoy taking care of my husband. I do not want to be "kept", babied, treated like I am incapable or anything like that. I am an independant woman, who happens to love being married. Is my husband perfect? Oh good Lord, no. But he is mine and I wouldn't change that for anything. I know I am going to ruffle a lot of feathers, but this whole equal rights thing is crap. A true Italian wife will agree with me.

There are things that I do not want to do and there are things that I want done for me. I want the door opened, I want my chair pulled out and I want my husband to take the lead. I do not want to change the oil in the car, I do not want to mow the lawn and I do not want to kill bugs. Trust me, there is a different between changing a man and training a man. HUGE difference.

I learned early on that my husband had certain things that needed to be changed. But those changes were never deal breakers. I had done my question asking during week one of dating. I knew I could not completely change him but I did know that I could train him to think the changes that needed to be made were his idea. You see how that works? Here is an example. When my husband was lacking in the romance department (Hey I got the hot Italian blood, I like romance) I started saying how lucky my friends were that their partners were planning date nights, bringing flowers to them, cooking them dinners. Now, you always have to preface how lucky I am to have a wonderful man like him, but…. Then poof...he planned a date night on his own. See, you plant the seed and voila!

After 25 years of marriage, sometimes I just have to throw my hands up and keep going. SInce I am a hot blooded, Italian woman, I have to be in charge. Rules are very important. So we do have rules in our marriage. Early on in our marriage, the rule was I was in charge of the inside of the house and my husband was in charge of the outside. Easy enough, right? Ugh, not really. About three years ago, my husband became obsessed with Storage Wars. He was instantly hooked. He started going to the auctions and was doing very well. In fact, he was even on the show. No lie. He then moved on to metal recycling. His obsession began to take over the entire outside of the house. In his head, he was in charge of the outside, so it was his to do with it what he wanted. Oh Lord, did he. The front yard holds his metal. The entrance to our home houses his storage treasures. The back yard table holds all the items that are stored in bins. My friends constantly tease me that I married Sanford, you know, Sanford and Son, the television show starring Redd Foxx and he was a junk collector. Some of my friends call my poor son, Lamont. There is literally, shit everywhere. I am a freaking saint. But it makes him happy. It works for us. He puts up with me and I put up with him. It is all about acceptance. 25 years. I don't need to say anymore.

After he collects all of the shit, excuse me, treasures, he has a garage sale. He has a customer list. He emails them and tells them about the garage sale. He even has a pre-sale the Thursday and Friday before the main sale. I swear, every older woman on his customer list, comes just to see him. He talks to them and treats them all special. When I give him a bathroom break or he has to go ref a game, they get really mad that he is not there. It cracks me up. What else can I do? The man makes money!! Who am I to argue?

He began doing youtube videos, documenting his words of wisdom. He makes videos about everything from metal recycling, to his experiences as a coach. He has even written two books. He amazes me everyday. I let him be who he wants to be. I can't change him so I live with it. But I will use it to my advantage. There is always something I want....

CHAPTER THREE - CHILDREN

There is no better mother than an Italian mother. Period!!
Calm down, I am so allowed to say that. Ask any Italian
mother and they will tell you the same thing. They will! We
love our children with everything we have in us and we
smother them until they cannot breathe. Why do we do that?
Because IT"S OUR JOB! I gave birth to two of the most
beautiful children in this world. They are so kind and loving.
My son is 20 and he still kisses me. My daughter is 23 and is
my best friend. They tell me everything. They tell me things I
really don't want to hear but I listen with an open mind and
heart and then I go scream into a pillow, come back out and
listen all over again. People tell me all the time how great my
children are. I am truly blessed. Younger couples ask us how
to raise their children because they want kids just like mine.
That is the biggest compliment any mother could ever want.
So how did we do it? Well here is my best advice. Take it or
leave it, I really don't care.

1. Always listen.
Don't ever looked shocked or appalled. Do not yell first and
listen later. You have to let your children know they can come
to you with anything. You are raising children to become

adults and you want them to have minds of their own. They are not clones of you. They are not always going to do the same things that you did. Look, I had the total Italian mother and I had the fear of God in me. I would never do anything wrong out of complete fear.

2. Put the fear of God in your children.

That is what the wooden spoon is for. Now, before you call CPS, relax. I do not believe in beating children, but let me ask you a simple question. When you were young and your mother could spank you, didn't you think twice about screwing up? My mother would say go ahead and call the police. I dare you. In todays world, the little shits do call the police. My mother broke a wooden spoon on my ass, and I never did whatever it was again. I turned out FINE.

3. Raise your children with total acceptance.

This is what you got. They did not ask to be born. You brought them into the world and it is your complete responsibility to see it through with unconditional love. The world is different today. Your kids are going to do things that we would have never considered.

4. Teach your children RESPECT.

Where is the respect now a days? I am a high school teacher and kids don't have respect. I truly feel when we took the power away from parents we gave children the go ahead to do whatever they wanted. There are no consequences. I cannot understand why parents fear their children. I will always be their parent first. When I say, "Because I say so" I mean it. Parents, you do not have to always tell your children WHY. It's OK.

5. Pick and choose your battles.

This is a huge one and I really struggle with this one, but it really helps your children's way into adulthood. When I lost my father 9 years ago, not only did it rock my world, it really crushed my children. They were so close to my dad. My daughter turned 18 and wanted a tattoo in honor of him. I was completely against tattoos. I fell into the stigma of what tattoos meant. They were not for good girls. I was very old fashioned when it came to that. But, how do I argue with my 18 year old daughter who wants to honor my father, her grandfather? I don't. I pick and choose my battles. She is not going to be any different the day after she gets the tattoo then she was the day before she got the tattoo. So, she got the tattoo. Then she got the next one. Then the next one. Now the Italian comes out in me and I say, fine as long as I can't see them on your wedding day. Well, I lost that one too. But they are beautiful and they make her who she is. They are important to her. Her brother has them too. Her and her brother have matching tattoos. So, being the type of parents we are, we wanted our children to know we will always be bound together, we got matching tattoos. All four of us have peace sign tattoos on our left wrists. I think it is the most beautiful thing we could have ever done. I have three and I will be getting one more. Probably when I sell my first book. That would be a kick!

6. When your child asks for help, get it for them. IT DOES NOT MAKE YOU A FAILURE.

The world is cruel. Children are faced with so much garbage everyday. If they have their own garbage to deal with on top of what they face is horrific. If you raise your daughter strong minded, she is a bitch. If your son is polite and respectful, he is gay. We as parents, need to teach our children acceptance. We were not put on this earth to judge each other. I worked at a Catholic school for 7 years and let me tell you, those kids were awful sometimes. If you did not play a sport and wanted to be on student council, you were a sissy. If your friend was the least bit sensitive, you must be gay. I just don't understand it. Why can't we raise our children to care about how they look and good grooming? Why can't our daughters choose abstinence and not be lesbian? I love the way my children have turned out and I would not trade my kids for any kid on the planet. Shouldn't every parent feel that way? God, I hope so.

7. Teach your children about finances early on.

This is a lesson I learned from my husband. We want our children to be financially independent. Start your children with a savings account at an early age. Yes, they should have fun and buy things that make them happy. But, they need to save the same amount for their future. We have encouraged them to buy property, another lesson from hubby. We want them to buy income producing assets like multi-unit apartment buildings. The biggest financial lesson we have taught them is to be their own boss and not have to work for anyone else.

8. They are equal, boy or girl.

I always have treated my children the same. It did not matter what sex they were, birth order, or anything. If one of them got five presents for Christmas, so did the other. I kept lists to make myself true to that. What we spent on my daughters sweet 16, the same was spent on my son's 16th birthday. What we will spend on my daughter's wedding, the same will be given to my son. They know that and we have kept to it. I truly think this has made them strong siblings. They would die for each other and they defend each other no matter what. We always say they are twins separated by three years. They know that no matter what happens to us, they will always have each other. It is all about family. Always.

9, & Infinity. Love them beyond.

Let them know that you will always be there for them, through the good and the bad. No matter what they do, you will be there. Unconditionally.

CHAPTER FOUR - SHOPPING

The sexiest thing I can do for my husband is not spend money. Save, save, save. That is all he preaches. I will tell you, if it was not for him, I would not be where I am today. I have a beautiful house, I am well provided for and I have a wonderful life. I am more of a live for today, we might die tomorrow kind of gal. We have a few dollars, let's take a trip. That's just me. He is very disciplined and he has gotten us to where we are today. For that, I will be eternally grateful. Now, he will tell you, one of the reasons he married me was because I shopped at Target and not Nordstroms. I love a deal. I will research for hours how to get the best deal and save the most money. When we take a trip, I scour for coupons deals. You can do more when you save more. Do I love to go out to eat? Absolutely. Do I love to cook for my family? More than words can say. I cut coupons, I shop the sales and I love Kohl's dollars. The .99 Cents Store is my heaven. I shop downtown Los Angeles and am proud to say that.

When you shop, you have to have a plan. I will go to three Ross Stores to find what I want. I will claw you down to get the last can of corn if it is on sale. It's for my family, what would you expect me to do? My mother is a shopper and is queen of the returns. I swear she will leave tags on things for a year just in case she decides she does not like it and wants to return it. She will argue with the sales clerk if it is past the 30 day return policy and by God she gets her money back. I learned from the best, what can I say?

When I pass a Mac counter, I truly crack up. These girls are in there paying huge amounts of money for the same thing I can buy at Target. Why do they do this? Because the media is telling them to do it. I have traveled to Italy on a few occasions and the women there are gorgeous. They can't hop in the car and run to the Mac counter. They put their whole heart and soul into natural beauty. They are loved for who they are, how they cook and how they take care of the ones they love. What a thought. Now, I must confess. I wear more make-up than the average Italian woman. But, when I am with family, it is all natural. They do not love me any less because of how I look, but how I love them.

I want to preach to the young girls of today. Be who you are not who the public wants you to be. My mother and father preached to me not to start using make-up, but unfortunately I did not listen. My daughter did not listen to me and now we are slaves to it. If I can help one young girl realize beauty comes from within, then I will sleep better. I want to bring the Italian way of thinking to the United States. I know I can do it. Then there is the matter of clothes…

I should be the spokesperson for Target. Seriously, they owe me millions. I look just as good as any housewife on TV and I do not shop at the huge department stores. It is all about education. See what is in style and head on over to Target and put some great outfits together. You will pay so much less and look just as good. Do I splurge sometimes? Absolutely. But I shop sales. Why should I put my hard earned money in someone else's pocket. It belongs in my pocket.

It is never too soon to teach your children about smart shopping. My kids are great. They shop the sales and don't fall into the "gotta haves". They save their money and buy what they need. They save for the fun stuff. They also know to save for their future. They both want to own homes and have started saving for down payments already. We have no problem with them living with us until they can afford to get their homes. Why would I want to kick them out? I want them with me as long as I can have them. I brought them into this world and I am no hurry to have them leave. It is all about family and love! My favorite times is when they are all home and we are together laughing, eating and sharing. Life is too short to not be together as much as possible.

CHAPTER FIVE - OVER EVERYTHING

Italians over cook, over eat, over plan and over love. There is nothing wrong with any of that! When I plan a dinner party, even it is for four, I cook for eight. You can never have too much. I would rather send people home with food then have someone hungry and not get enough to eat. You can always eat it the next day. Right? I cook with love. I want the people visiting to feel like they are the most important people in my home. I plan every last detail. One of my favorite things to do is set the table. I love to theme my dinner parties down to the napkins. The food has to flow with the occasion and the dessert has to be the grand finale. Wine plays a huge part in the dinner. I always serve good Italian wine. Italians know wine. You never want the wine to over power the dinner.

My friends tease me that every party I plan is an event. The running joke is you do not want to miss one of Pam's events. I laugh. If they only knew how much I love to entertain, they would understand they are doing me a favor. I take months to plan every last detail. From the time they enter, I want them to feel a part of the event and know the theme I am going for. In fact, that will be my next book. I am going to teach you how to plan a full course, fully decorated, fully entertaining party for 180 people for $3750.00. It can be done. You will have to buy the book. It will be worth every penny. But moving on... As I write this book, I am in the process of planning my daughter's wedding. There are days that I am so excited to do things in regards to the wedding and there are other days that I sit and cry. I don't tell her that because I want this to be the happiest day of her life. Like I have previously shared, I have two amazing children. We are very close. I put the brakes on any fights and make them talk things out and move on. When their father and I go to heaven (because that is where all good Italians go) they will always have each other. I want them to be close and be in each others lives. This will allow me to die peacefully. So, on certain days I cry when thinking about the wedding because we will no longer be under the same roof. Thank God we love the new son-in-law. It would be hell if we did not. He loves our daughter the way she deserves to be loved and what more could we want. He is a nice Italian boy (not a prerequisite, but a plus). He blends into our family and we already view him as a son. I don't butt into their business unless they are wrong. I am laughing. No seriously, I don't. In regards to the wedding, I have chosen to do everything that my daughter and he wants. Even if I think it is silly, ugly or dumb, I tell her it is your day and you will have what you want as I bleed inside. What do you mean you do not want rhinestones on your centerpieces? Are you sure you do not want to wear a crown attached to your veil? You want to wear converse with your wedding dress?? Again, bleeding inside. But, this is the woman I raised to have a mind of her own and to be strong. That she is! So, maybe I too, shall wear Converse with my fully beaded gown and tiara.

CHAPTER 6 - WITH THE WEDDING COMES IN-LAWS

I am so thankful that my daughter is marrying into a family that is so incredibly good to her. She will gain four sisters, a brother, one sister-in-law and four brother-in-laws. She will gain a mother and father-in-law who already love her and treat her as a member of their family. I could not ask for anything more. They are a blended family and you would never know it. They all love each other and accept each other. That is all I ever wanted and did not get. She is so blessed to be getting that.

Another thing I have learned is to accept all of my daughter and son-in-laws decisions. I keep having to remind my Italian mother that it is their life. They have to experience the good, the bad and the ugly. To my mom's credit, she always wanted to make things easy for me. She wanted to prevent me from getting hurt. What she did not understand is that is the way I learned. My daughter knows that we are always there for her and for her husband.

The saddest thing for a young married couple is acceptance. As an in-law, we need to remember that. We are not always going to agree, but for the sake of our children, we have to compromise. I will never do anything to lose my children. When they get married, I want to be excited over gaining more children and grandchildren. Making the circle bigger is gratifying and they have to know that we will respect them no matter what. I want family dinners to get bigger and louder! My biggest joy is family dinner and to get along and include in-laws is just another added joy.

I try so hard not to be judgmental. Everyone has the right to live their life as they feel fit. Who am I to judge someone else's decisions? That includes my future son-in-law and my someday daughter-in-law. Now, don't get me wrong. If my children are being hurt physically or mentally, you can bet money I will be the first one to step in. They are still my babies and don't forget it. But, they have to learn on their own. I have to respect that. And I will.

I will be writing an advice book for in-laws soon after this book. I just think it is so important to start out on the right foot. I have to say it, but a son will choose his wife over his family 80% of the time. The other 20% are momma's boys!

CHAPTER 7 – MAKE THE CIRCLE SMALLER

When we are young, we base our popularity on the number of friends we have. Are they really friends? I think not. People have come and gone in my life and I really do not care. I used to. Not so much now. I now don't care about popularity but I do care about loyalty. I learned a lot from the movie "Meet the Fockers." Not the spying part or the control part, but the circle of trust part. Be very careful about who you let into your circle. I have been burned and hurt so many times. It comes with the whole Italian mom thing. We think we can fix everyone and that everyone needs me. I needed to reverse my thinking to who I need. I need people that have a vested interest in me and who treat my family with respect and kindness. The friends I have now are lifetime friends. They are my family and I treat them that way. Do not lie to me. Do not use me. I am guilty of letting people in too quickly. Now I am very selective. Loyalty is huge. Have the common decency to tell me to my face. I am a big girl and I wear big girl panties. I can take it. I now can step back and take criticism. My number one rule of friendship is to NEVER judge parenting or tell a parent how to be a parent. I only share advice when it is asked for. I may think you are crazy and I may not agree with how you handle your children, but it is not my business and I am not God, I do not judge.

Being a parent is the hardest job in the world. I am by no means perfect, I can only do what I know is best for me and my family. You can only do what works for you. I can just give advice. YOU have to ask for it. It took a long time for me to learn that I am not obligated to be your friend. I only want to be around people who bring me up not put me down. That was another hard lesson to learn. I did not want to hurt people. So, I took people being unloyal and nasty because I felt like I had to stay their friend. Now, with the friends I have, I know what true friendship is. They accept me for who I am. I have been called the female Howard Stern and I am OK with that. I should be able to voice my opinions and thoughts without stepping on eggshells. They also must be able to do the same. I now can say that my friends are my family and I say it with pride. I am proud of who I have surrounded myself with. I have to be an example to my children so they pick wonderful people to surround themselves with. I am proud to say they have.

My son has mastered this. Not to say he has not been hurt along the way. He is very selective and has had his trued friends since kindergarten. My daughter also has remarkable friends. One is also since kindergarten. You know a true friend when you don't talk for months and you can just pick up where you left off. They don't make you feel guilty for not seeing them or spending time. They understand that life is busy. What a beautiful thing.

I was the first to get married amongst my friends. The amount of guilt that was put on me because I could not go out with them was so hurtful. I had a baby and that was my priority. But when they had kids, the universe revolved around them. Understanding, I am just saying!

CHAPTER 8 – WHERE DO WE GO FROM HERE?

Am I the only Italian mother out there? NO! But I will speak up and I am proud to do so. I have no problem if you do not agree with me. In fact, I would be worried if everyone always agreed with me. I have no problem stating the truth. I do have a problem with people thinking that their way is the only way. I want people of all nationalities to step up and say all learn from each other. My way of thinking is mine. I own it. I can only wish that it helps others in their families. We stop learning when we stop listening. Moms have to support each other and surround themselves with other support systems out there. Plus, when you all realize that my way is the best way, your lives will be so much easier! That is why I am starting this series. There will be so much more.

Visit my youtube Channel – The Italian Mom

The Italian Mom is a mom first and foremost. She lives in the Los Angeles County with her husband of 25 years and her two beautiful children plus a soon to be son-in-law. She is 48 years young and has learned through her 2 visits to Italy to live life passionately and truthfully and not give a shit what others think. She has a Bachelor's Degree in Liberal Studies and a Master's Degree in Reading Curriculum. She will be adding many books to this series to help others understand that there are many ways to do many things. She is just presenting one way in her own voice. This is just the beginning of many things to come. Caio!

Future Series will include:

How to throw a party for 180 guests for $3750.00 the Italian Way

The Italian Wedding

Italian Moms Unite

Visiting the Mother Land

My Youtube channel will feature videos on all subject matters above, plus interviews, cooking and a whole lot more.

26958988R10023

Made in the USA
San Bernardino, CA
06 December 2015